EMERALD JOURNEY

A Walk through Northwest Gardens

Written and Photographed by Carolyn Starner

Greenstem Press

Library of Congress Control Number 2004100602

ISBN 0-9748901-0-3

Published by Greenstem Press
1907 East Desmet Avenue
Spokane, Washington 99202
509-939-1906
e-mail: Greenstem@comcast.net

Printed in Korea by Amica International Inc.
844 Industry Drive
Seattle, WA 98188
206-575-2740
e-mail: amica@ix.netcom.com

ACKNOWLEDGEMENTS

I acknowledge the following for their support, cooperation and permissions in the production of Emerald Journey. Thank you for your many kindnesses.

Oregon State Parks Department
City of Eugene Department of Parks and Open Space
The Friends of Deepwood
Portland Parks and Recreation
Portland Classical Chinese Garden, copyright owner of their images, used with permission
The Japanese Garden Society of Portland
Lakewold Gardens
Metro Parks Tacoma
Weyerhaeuser Company, owner of Pacific Rim Bonsai Collection, copyright owner of their images, used with permission
Rhododendron Species Foundation
Seattle Department of Parks and Recreation
University of Washington
The Arbor Fund
City of Bellevue Parks and Community Services Department
Washington State Parks Department
Spokane Park and Recreation Department
Vancouver Park Board
Park and Tilford Shopping Center and Gardens
Butchart Gardens
Royal Roads University
Minter Gardens
Eastside Librarians, Spokane, Washington
Jessie Quintero Johnson, copyreader

CONTENTS

GARDENS OF OREGON STATE

GARDENS OF WASHINGTON STATE

GARDENS OF BRITISH COLUMBIA

To the gardeners, administrators, volunteers, friends
and patrons who make these gardens possible
and
to those who gave encouragement for this project.

PREFACE

The gardens of the Northwest are loosely held in a common bond by climate and location. At the same time, they are as diverse as the gardeners who have designed and nurtured them. These gardeners have drawn inspiration from cultures throughout the world to create a potpourri of stunning gems. To walk in these gardens is to experience an amalgamation of diverse backgrounds and turns of events.

Because of this diversity, one never tires of returning again and again. Each visit offers a new gift, a new idea, a new opportunity to experience the aesthetics, rhythms, and balances of garden design. It is my hope that your garden walks will refresh and excite you. It is my hope that you will take the essence of your garden walks back to your own gardens, and that you will inspire and influence others with your own unique interpretation of what you have seen.

It is also my hope that Emerald Journey will further the nurturing connection between gardens everywhere and those who visit them. Gardens nurture us with beauty, inspiration and soul comfort. They teach color, pattern, texture and scale of plants. They excite us with undreamed of plant combinations, delight us with new varieties, and transport us with their fragrance. And we, in return, nurture the gardens by volunteering our time, labor, knowledge and monetary support, and by the care we take when we visit them. Because most of the gardens that are open to the public depend on our help, it is my hope that we will all do what we can to preserve them.

SHORE ACRES GARDENS
Coos Bay, Oregon

Because they lay in ruin for years before being resurrected, Shore Acres Gardens are sometime called "the ghost gardens". Originally a 1900's summer estate for lumber baron, Louis J. Simpson, the home fell into disrepair and was burned and bulldozed in the 1940's. The derelict gardens lay forgotten until 1971 when the Oregon State Park staff began a reconstruction project that restored them to their former glory.

The largest section in the gardens is the Formal Garden with geometric, boxwood bordered flower beds. Awesomely beautiful on its own, it is even more beautiful in the setting of a rugged coastal forest. At the far end of the Formal Garden, one enters a serene Oriental Stroll Garden with a central lily pond. Beyond this is an AARS Rose Display Garden. At the ocean's edge, where the mansion once stood, is a glass enclosed observation room with a 180° view of the picturesque coastline.

Title Page, Opposite, and Above *The largest garden at Shore Acres is the meticulously groomed Formal Garden. Brick and aggregate concrete paths intersect boxwood edged beds filled with a savvy mix of annuals, perennials and shrubs. Cookies and hot cider are served in the garden cottage each winter during the seasonal light display.*

Opposite Bottom Left *Rosa "Brandy". The AARS Rose Display Garden is just beyond the Oriental Garden. Visiting a rose garden gives one the opportunity to view a huge selection of varieties and to check out fragrances before making purchases for your own garden.*

Opposite Bottom Right Several large *beds of dahlias awe visitors with their never-ending shapes, sizes and colors. Their bright oranges, pinks, reds and purples light up the garden from mid-summer until the first frosts of fall.*

Opposite and Above Left *At the far end of the Formal Garden is an Oriental Stroll Garden. The oval lily pond is surrounded by Japanese maples, pines, ferns, hostas and rhododendrons.*

Opposite Bottom Left *A bank of white hydrangeas line this path to the Oriental and Rose Gardens.*

Above Right *The former two-story, 224 foot long estate house once stood on the edge of these cliffs. Early in the morning when the foggy mists are drifting across the dripping arms of the overhanging cypress and the mournful cry of seals encircles the garden, one can understand why Mrs. Simpson sometimes felt isolated here.*

OWEN ROSE GARDEN
Eugene, Oregon

Even if you have never visited a rose garden, you will want to visit the Owen Rose Garden just to see the majestic old Tartarian Cherry tree that dominates the main garden. Planted in the 1860's, this tree stands guard over five acres of All-American Selections roses on the banks of the Willamette River. The garden, which was established in 1951, is entered through a curving sweep of pergolas that support old-fashioned climbing roses. Many mature trees, including magnolias and conifers, give the garden a pleasant sense of enclosure. The Eugene Parks and Recreation Department maintains the garden with the assistance of the Eugene Rose Society.

Above *The Tartarian Cherry tree.*

Left *The Owen Rose Garden in late spring.*

Above Left *A path meanders through the many beautiful trees in the garden.*

Above Right *The garden boasts two pergolas that support climbing plants. This sturdy rose covered pergola welcomes guests from the parking area. The newer pergola, built by the city of Eugene and the Eugene Delta Rotary Club, is constructed of green metal rods and disks that arch gracefully through space.*

Opposite Top *A close up look at the aging Tartarian Cherry. Its successor grows near by.*

Right and Opposite bottom *Garden scenes and a magnolia tree.*

HENDRICK'S PARK RHODODENDRON GARDEN
Eugene, Oregon

Nestled within Hendrick's Park's 77 acres of 300 year old Douglas fir trees lies an internationally recognized 12 acre rhododendron garden. This impeccable gem was founded in 1951. Through the efforts of the American Rhododendron Society and the Eugene Parks Department, rhododendron enthusiasts have gathered some 6,000 plants, highlighting rhododendrons, azaleas, magnolias and viburnums. Some they cultivated themselves, others were collected from as far away as England, China and Japan. The plants are arranged under a canopy of white oaks, flowering trees and shrubs.

Opposite Top Left *Basalt pillars form a natural sculpture on either side of the garden's entrance.* Opposite Top Right and This Page Right *Benches are placed throughout the garden for resting, for small discussion groups on tour, or just to pause and enjoy the quiet beauty of the garden.*

Opposite Bottom Left *The main walk in the Rhododendron Garden is dominated by the wild beauty of these Oregon white oaks racing across a broad expanse of lawn.* Center *Lush plantings of groundcovers, one sign of a mature garden, supply a delightful variety of year round color, pattern and texture.* Right *One of many color combinations found in rhododendron flowers.*

Above *The many trails in the garden provide excellent views of the lush plantings.*

THE BUSH HOUSE
AND ROSE GARDEN
Salem, Oregon

Bush House, The centerpiece of a 100 acre gentleman's estate, was completed in 1878 and was occupied by the Bush family until 1953. Placed on the National Registrar of Historic Places in 1974, the impeccably maintained Victorian home is open to the public. Many of the original technical features, wallpapers, and furnishings are still in place.

Original fruit and ornamental trees still grace the landscape, as does the original Bush Conservatory, built in 1882. The Bush collection of Old Garden Roses is one of the finest in the Pacific Northwest. Some of the roses were planted by the Bush family. Many others were collected from local farmsteads and pioneer homes. Identifying these old roses is an ongoing process. Bush Gardens welcomes input. The sometimes imaginative names are included in parenthesis on their labels.

Previous Page Left *The 1878 Bush House, beautifully restored and lovingly cared for, is open for public viewing.* Right *A formal accent in the Rose Garden.*

Above *The perfect spot to rest after the eternal search for your favorite rose.*

Left *A late summer floral arrangement in the flower beds surrounding the greenhouse.*

Opposite Top Left *Magnolia grandiflora grows in zones 7-9. Its large, cup-shaped, creamy white flowers are fragrant and grow to 10 inches across.*

Opposite Top Right *Rosa 'Duet' is a vigorous hybrid tea rose with double flowers in 2 shades of pink. 'Duet' thrives in zones 5-9 and makes a good cut flower. The bush is 4-5 feet tall.*

Opposite Bottom *One area of the extensive rose garden.*

HISTORIC DEEPWOOD ESTATE
Salem, Oregon

Deepwood house is one of Salem's most striking examples of Queen Anne architecture. Designed by architect William C. Knight and built in 1894, it's graceful Victorian features are topped with steep gabled peaks.

Oregon's first female landscape architects, Edith Schryver and Elizabeth Lord, began designing the garden with owner, Alice Brown, in 1929. Their mutual goal was to create a Northwest garden that captured the elusive quality of peace and easiness found in old English gardens. The "felt" quality they called "charm" is evident today throughout the 5½ acres of intertwining gardens, woodland walks and garden structures.

Left *The front entrance to beautiful Deepwood house is surrounded by a sweeping lawn with shade trees that predate the home.* **Above** *The gazebo on the west side of the house was once a viewing area at one end of the tennis court. A solarium jutting off the porch also serves as a shady summer room.*

Above Left *Clematis envelop the side entrance to the Moon Garden.*

Above Right *A rose covered trellis arch frames an enticing view of the teahouse in the Moon Garden. The lattice fence, intersecting brick paths and boxwood hedges give formal structure to the garden.*

Opposite Top *A pleasing mix of azaleas and ferns border one side of the central lawn behind the house. A white 1905 gazebo, backed by a massive clipped holly hedge, stands in the distance.*

Opposite Bottom Left *The Moon Garden is so called because the shimmer of its pastel colored moonlit plants invite an evening visit.*

Opposite Bottom Right *The carriage house on the East side of the house is a reminder of quieter times. The upper floor was often used to house outdoor help.*

Above *Alice Brown had this garden designed for her marriage to Keith Powell in 1945. The scrolled boxwood repeats the design in the iron fence bordering the garden. This garden is gradually being renovated.*

Opposite Top Left *Formally clipped boxwood forms an aisle to the white painted iron gazebo, the perfect setting for an outdoor wedding.*

Opposite Bottom Left *Iris from the garden near the greenhouse. Bulbs, annuals and perennials envelop the East side of the property with an informal display of old fashioned flowers.*

Opposite Right *The formal English gardens are bordered on the west side by Rita Steiner Fry Nature Trail, a woodland walk where native trees, shrubs and wildflowers meander along Pringle Creek.*

CRYSTAL SPRINGS
RHODODENDRON GARDEN
Portland, Oregon

Each spring more than 2,500 rhododendrons and azaleas burst into bloom along the winding wooded pathways of Crystal Springs Rhododendron Garden. This magnificent display of color is further enhanced by the sparkling blue waters of spring-fed Crystal Springs Lake.

Established in 1950, this unique seven acre garden has become a highly successful cooperative effort between the city of Portland and the Portland chapter of The American Rhododendron Society.

Previous Left *Crystal Springs Rhododendron Garden surrounds a lagoon with colorful blooms.*

Previous Right *A small water cascade adds pleasing music to this narrow lakeside garden.*

Above *This area of the garden gives double pleasure with flowering rhododendrons on one side and a lake with cavorting wildlife on the other.*

Right *This lucky duck lives at Crystal Springs.*

Opposite Top *A large area of lawn serves as a foil to the riot of colorful blooms that encircle it each spring.*

Opposite Bottom Left *These geese are one of the 94 species of birds that frequent the garden.* Right *The dramatic entrance bridges the Jane Martin Waterfall Garden.*

PORTLAND CLASSICAL CHINESE GARDEN
Portland, Oregon

With just 15 years passing from inception to completion, a Portland parking lot was transformed into the largest authentic urban Suzhou-style Chinese garden outside China. This feat is a tribute to the dedication, steadfastness and cooperation of the citizens of Portland and its sister city, Suzhou. With the guidance of design teams from both cities, Suzhou craftsmen built the garden using skills that have been perfected for thousands of years.

As with Portland's Chinese garden, traditional gardens of suzhou were built in the city on small areas of land. Unlike Portland's garden, the traditional gardens were not places to visit. They were places to live. Owned by successful private citizens, they were built with a number of living spaces surrounding an inner garden with a lake as the central feature. Along with architecture and water, rocks and plants were the other necessary elements in the gardens. Used together in the Suzhou style, they form an astonishingly beautiful garden meant to calm the spirit and soothe the senses.

The Tower of Cosmic Reflections teahouse offers a high overlook of the garden. The Moon-locking pavilion on the bridge acts as a resting place where one watches for the reflection of the moon on the lake. The light wings and pointed corners of the roof are a perfect example of the delicate and beautiful Suzhou style of architecture

Above *The Hall of Brocade Clouds, the receiving hall where guests are entertained, has open views to the garden on all four sides.*

Left *A chestnut-colored corridor with fret-work balustrades floats over the pond*

Above *A moon gate frames the scholar's courtyard. The courtyard, as well as the scholar's study across the courtyard, are reserved for the master of the household. They serve as a place to read, paint, write poetry, or just think. The courtyard floor is made by hand-setting small oval stones to form a repeating floral pattern. This pattern is called "plum blossoms on cracked ice". The white walls, gray stone and slate, and the chestnut colored wood comprise the color scheme of the architecture.*

Above *Tracery windows set into the walls introduce an intricate interplay between solids and spaces.*

Left and Right *A pair of Chinese foo dogs traditionally guard the entrance to the garden. They are actually lions, but, because they resemble a Pekingese, they are commonly referred to as dogs.*

Opposite Page *A small entry court, the courtyard of tranquility, welcomes the visitor with a simply but elegantly planted corner garden. A large Taihu rock acts as a natural sculpture. High white walls are used to enclose the garden.*

Above Left *A water cave constructed of Taihu rockery adds depth to the garden. The musical dimension of water masks the sounds of the surrounding city.*

Above Right *Rocks, plants and architecture in a simple yet complex combination. The tracery window offers a tantalizing peek into another courtyard. The clay roof is edged with decorative tiles that direct rainwater.*

Opposite Page *Covered corridors are links between the buildings and the garden. The fretwork adds visual interest, making the structure appear light and delicate. The subdued colors denote simplicity and good taste.*

Above *Hand-carved foo dogs act as decorative finials on a balustrade.*

WASHINGTON PARK INTERNATIONAL ROSE TEST GARDEN
Portland, Oregon

Given that Portland has been called the 'City of Roses' since the early 1900's, its not surprising that it is home to the oldest official, continuously operated public rose test garden in the United States. The five acre garden, designed on three levels down a hillside, serves as a testing ground for the All-American Rose Selections, the American Rose Society, and foreign hybridists. The site is beautifully landscaped with wide brick paths and stairways, fountains and sculptures. Mt. Hood and the Cascades can be seen in the distance.

Adjacent to the Rose Garden is an intimate Shakespearean Garden planted with perennials, wildflowers, shrubs and trees mentioned in Shakespeare's plays.

Preceding Page *A metal sculpture adds structure and beauty to the garden.*

Above *Rosa 'Whiskey Mac', a hybrid tea rose with rounded, double, fragrant, light amber-yellow flowers.*

Left *Flowers growing in the Shakespearean Garden.*

Opposite Top *A gazebo provides a view of the three tiers of roses in the garden, the perfect observation point on a rainy day.*

Opposite Bottom Left *Rosa 'Dainty Bess' a branching hybrid tea rose with scented, pale pink flowers.*

Opposite Bottom Right *Rosa 'Little Artist', a neat upright miniature rose with semi-double red flowers.*

THE JAPANESE GARDEN OF PORTLAND
Portland, Oregon

On the west side of Washington Park, just above the International Rose Test Garden, lies one of the most authentic Japanese gardens outside of Japan. The 5 ½ acre site was designed by Professor Takuma Tono, then head of Landscape Architecture at Tokyo Agricultural University. The garden opened to the public in 1967. It is comprised of five Japanese garden styles: the Flat Garden (Hira-niwa), the Strolling Pond Garden (Chisen-Kaiyui-Shiki), the Tea Garden (Roji-niwa), the Natural Garden (Shukeiyen), and the Sand and Stone Garden (Seki-Tei). All five gardens are serene places that promote reflection and contemplation.

Previous Page Left *The open covered porch of the Japanese pavilion faces the Flat Garden, or hiraniwa. The flat sea of raked sand is planted with a cup and gourd, symbolizing pleasure and happiness.*

Previous Page Right *The simple, functional beauty of Japanese design is reflected in the material used for this walkway.*

Above *Foo dogs are placed on either side of the entry as protectors of the garden.*

Opposite Top *Those who choose to walk up to the main entrance rather than ride the tram, enter through these antique gates. The path winds up the hillside through a wooded shade garden of maples, ferns, rhododendrons, ivy and hosta. This area acts as a quieting transition between the busy street and the serenity of the garden.*

Opposite Bottom Left *The Iyo Stone near the Flat Garden.* Right *The functional yet artistic use of texture at the edge of the Sand and Stone Garden shows the mark of a highly trained eye.*

Above *The plants at the Japanese Garden are artfully placed to show off their shapes, colors and textures.*

Opposite Top *A view of the imposing five story pagoda from the wisteria arbor. The pagoda is a gift from Sapporo, Japan, Portland's Sister City. The layered squares contain the five stories of light. Above are the circles of heaven capped by a lotus blossom.*

Opposite Bottom *Curved branches form unique gate handles. Stone lanterns are primarily used as sculptural pieces in Japanese gardens, although candles are sometimes placed in them to set a mood or to provide a dim light for a pathway.* Left *A lantern near the pavilion with a view of the Portland sky line and Mt. Hood.* Center *A snow lantern sits at a bend in a stone path. The rough-surfaced meander causes these who pass to slow down physically and then mentally.* Right *A simple stone lantern at the edge of the waterfall pond.*

Above Left *A small stream runs from the Strolling Pond Garden to the Iris Garden. Its edges are filled with plants selected for variations of texture, shape and color. At the far end of the stream is a two-legged kotoji lantern with one foot on land and one foot in the water.*

Above Right *A waterfall near the Iris Garden. The pond of koi and the sound of water causes visitors to slow their pace.*

Opposite Top *The Moon Bridge (not a full moon) spans the Strolling Pond Garden. Japanese gardens of this type have a pond as their main feature. Vistas are viewed across the pond as one moves along the path.*

Opposite Bottom Left *The Iris Water Garden is traversed by crossing the zig-zag bridge, or yatsuhashi, that weaves its way through a pond of iris. It is said that if you quickly jump to one side when you come to a turn in the bridge, you will lose any evil spirits that may be following you. They are simply caught by surprise and fall off the end.* Right *A large willow tree shades those who pause on this side path for a view across the strolling pond garden.*

PENINSULA PARK ROSE GARDEN
Portland, Oregon

 Originally opened in 1913, the formal rose garden at Peninsula Park was Portland's first public rose garden. The two acre garden, which is six feet below street level, is surrounded by a balustrade with broad sweeping stairways leading to the garden below. Reminiscent of the French parterre gardens, the rectangular layout is a symmetrical arrangement of boxwood enclosed rose beds separated by wide brick and concrete walkways that converge on a quatrefoil shaped pool with a fountain at its center. Each corner of the garden is accented by four pollarded catalpa trees. The original gazebo-like bandstand, a Portland Historic Landmark, overlooks the garden.

When designing Peninsula Park, the city of Portland included a beautiful formal rose garden with an octagonal shaped bandstand in their plans. In the early 1900's when the park was constructed, neighborhood parks were the center for social activities. Recorded music was not widely available so families would gather at the park to picnic, socialize and listen to the bands that played there. The showplace of its time, the rose garden received 300,000 visitors the first year. Mme. Caroline Testout, the official Portland rose, is still grown there.

LAKEWOLD
Tacoma, Washington

From the time that Cory and Eulalie Wagner made Lakewold their home in 1938 until they donated the property to The Friends of Lakewold in 1987, Mrs. Wagner carefully tended her garden to perfection. With the help of Thomas Church, a renowned American landscape architect, the property was gradually transformed into a cohesive but diverse number of formal and informal gardens. They include a Rhododendron Collection of over five hundred varieties, a formal Lawn garden with a teahouse, a Woodland Garden, a Rose Garden and a Knot Garden. Several old garden sculptures, placed appropriately throughout the property, add a breathtaking touch to almost every garden, as do the mature collection of Japanese maples, camellias, and cherry trees.

Lakewold, one of America's great estate gardens, will draw you back again and again with its views of Gravely Lake and Mount Rainier, its peaceful atmosphere, and its beauty.

Previous Page Left *The Parterre Garden just off the sunroom is in a formal style adopted from old French gardens. Neatly trimmed, low boxwood hedges form geometric patterns in which flowers are grown. The topiary animals are used to accent the design.*

Previous Page Right *A sculptural fragment decorates a pathway. Many fine old sculptures, collected over the years, grace the property. Garden decoration adds interest to a garden and helps to define it's style. Take care when purchasing gazing balls, birdbaths, weathervanes, large decorative pots, furniture and other garden items. They should support the theme of the garden and add continuity to the plan.*

Above and Opposite *The Gazebo Teahouse is the terminus of a long brick walkway leading from the house. Both were built in 1922. The walkway, a herringbone pattern of brick laid in sand, has endured with few repairs. The Teahouse, used for entertaining family friends in summer, has been remodeled several times. The curved shape in the floor repeats the pattern of the quatrefoil pool nearby. Vines will eventually cover the dome to provide additional shade.*

Above Left and Right *Across the courtyard at the homes entryway are a pair of sculptures, each on their own pedestal under a flowering tree. Although his weapon is at rest, he is obviously aiming for her heart. She coyly pretends not to notice.*

Opposite Top *The Georgian style home was remodeled by the Wagners in the 1950's by architects William and Geoffrey. The rhododendron cartouche above the entrance is a reflection of the Rhododendron 'Bow Bell' planted near by.*

Opposite Bottom Left *Rhododendron 'Hotei' is one of the 500 varieties of rhododendron planted at Lakewold. Grown mostly for their spectacular flowers, they bloom mainly during April and May in the Northwest. Some have hot colors and a strong spicy fragrance.*

Opposite Bottom Right *A deep red peony grows in the perennial beds near the house.*

Opposite top and Bottom Left *Knot gardens are best planted where they can be seen from a raised terrace or a window. This view is from a second story window. A planting style that was particularly popular in the 16th century, the beds are laid out in a formal, sometimes complex, pattern formed with dwarf hedges or herbs. Green Teucrium and gray Santolina are used to form the ribbons in this knot.*

Opposite Bottom Right *Picnic Lookout sports a grand view of Gravelly Lake.*

Above Left *Carved wooden owls in a woodland setting.*

Above Right *A lovely old elephant sculpture graces a small patio on one side or the house.*

Left *One of a pair of sculptures near the pool.*

W. W. SEYMOUR BOTANICAL CONSERVATORY
Tacoma Washington

A gift to the city of Tacoma from W. W. Seymour, and one of only three Victorian conservatories still standing on the west coast, the Seymour conservatory is built in a coveted design featuring a twelve-sided central dome. The newly renovated structure, with more than 12,000 panes of glass, houses permanent displays as well as displays of seasonal and holiday interest. The permanent display of 200 species of tropical plants includes ornamental figs, tropical fruit trees, bird of paradise, cacti and bromeliads. The unique exotic sculptures and a tropical waterfall pond serve to transport visitors to a distant jungle atmosphere.

In the Victorian period when plantsmen were on a quest to discover and bring home exotic plants from around the world, many cities and wealthy private citizens built conservatories to accommodate their discoveries. Over time the escalating cost of maintenance and heating caused the demise of many of the conservatories. Only three structures from this period still stand on the West Coast today. Although most of these beautiful old structures are gone, there is a renewed interest in building with glass. With the economy of construction afforded by new materials and building techniques, conservatories are once again feasible.

POINT DEFIANCE PARK GARDENS
Tacoma, Washington

Seven-hundred acre Point Defiance Park spreads its lush greenery across a blunt curve of land that nudges the waters of Puget Sound. Originally set aside as a military reservation, it was never used for this purpose. In the late 1800's, settlers of the area recognized the potential of the point and asked President Grover Cleveland to designate the area as a public park. Five-hundred acres remain forested and undeveloped except for trails that allow visitors to enjoy the awesome variety of beautiful old trees and the watery views across island-dotted Puget Sound.

The gardens of Point Defiance lie just inside the main Pearl Street entrance. Low, rose entwined pergolas cover paths leading to sweeping beds of annuals, perennials and the Dahlia Garden. A beautiful Rose Garden encircles a large gazebo with fragrance and color, providing a romantic spot for weddings and other special celebrations of life.

Other gardens include a five acre Pacific Northwest Native Plants Garden featuring native plants in a variety of habitats, and Rhododendron, Herb and Iris Gardens. A serene Japanese Garden surrounds a 1914 Pagoda. Refurbished in 1988, the Pagoda is now used for meetings, receptions and weddings.

Previous Page Left *Hot perennials, backed by flowering shrubs and tempered by the cool leaves of Dusty Miller, swing onto the lawn for dramatic effect. This display may tempt gardeners with a two-foot deep flower fringe around their lawns to forsake some grass for the deep beds required for this luscious combination of shrubs, perennials and annuals.*

Previous Page Right *Maidenhair fern.*

Above *A simple pergola covered with climbing roses.*

Opposite Top *The sturdy gazebo in the Rose Garden is the beautiful site of many weddings. Royal Sunset, a fragrant climber, frames the scene.*

Opposite Bottom *Some of the many varieties of dahlias that are grown near the Rose Garden. Dahlias range in hot colors from white to red, orange to yellow and pink to dark purple with blooms from two to over ten inches across.*

Opposite Top *A bright display of impatiens backed by hydrangeas frames a pergola of separate parts that read as a whole.*

Opposite Bottom Left *Rhododendron Glen.*

Opposite Bottom Right *A mixed border of annuals and perennials is given structure and enclosure with hedges and arbors.*

Above and Left *The Japanese Garden at Point Defiance Park surrounds a 1914 Pagoda style building that serves as a meeting and reception hall. The front garden is a quiet contemplation garden under a canopy of old trees. A tori gate welcomes one to the rear garden, a stroll garden with a pond.*

RHODODENDRON SPECIES BOTANICAL GARDENS
Federal Way, Washington

The Rhododendron Species Botanical Gardens house over 4,500 forms of more than 488 species on its beautiful 24 acre woodland setting at Weyerhaeuser Company's corporate headquarters. A species rhododendron is one that is found in the wild or came from the wild originally, as opposed to hybrids cultivated by nurserymen.

Plantings of ferns, primroses, iris, heather, maples, magnolias, and conifers grow under the canopy of native forest as companion plants to the rhododendrons. Besides the flourish of pink, yellow, white, red and violet blooms in spring, the garden boasts a vivid display of brilliant color from the Japanese maples each fall. Stands of bamboo, reeds and grasses provide landing and hiding places for the dragonflies, frogs and other water life at the pond. An Alpine Garden and lookout gazebo are near the center of the garden.

Opposite Top *Over 10,000 Rhododendrons grow in the Rhododendron Species Botanical Gardens, one of the finest collections in the world. Shown is Rhododendron oreodoxa.*

Opposite Bottom Left *Trillium, a native North American woodland plant, flourishes in the moist shady garden.*

Opposite Bottom Right *One of the many delights of a woodland garden are the unexpected surprises of beauty, such as this lovely root pattern with autumn leaves.*

Above Left *A bench by the pond offers a fine close-up view of pond life, as well as a distant view of the lookout gazebo at the crest of the Alpine Garden.*

Above Right *The gazebo provides a fine view of the compact rhododendrons and high country plants growing amongst the scree and rocky outcrops of the hillside.*

PACIFIC RIM BONSAI COLLECTION

Federal Way, Washington

Nestled under a tall canopy of Douglas fir, The Pacific Rim Bonsai Collection is displayed in an outdoor gallery adjacent to the Rhododendron Species Foundation. The collection of 50 bonsai was conceived by the Weyerhaeuser Company in 1989 to honor ties with the Pacific Rim Nations and to celebrate the Washington State Centennial.

Bonsai is a horticultural expression of a fine art first practiced as penjing in China during the Han and Qin Dynasties (221 BC – 220 AD). Each generation of artists used the expertise of previous generations and contributed its own innovation of style and interpretation. The practice of penjing eventually spread to Japan where it was called bonsai, a planting in a shallow container that creates a mood and suggests a scene other than itself.

Healthy deciduous or evergreen plants that are long-lived and indigenous to the area where they will be grown make the best bonsai. Styles of bonsai include formal or informal upright, slanting, semi-cascade, cascade, and group plantings called forests or groves. A well-balanced collection such as the Pacific Rim Collection uses these forms in a variety of plants that provide interest in every season.

Left *Most of the unique Bonsai in the Pacific Rim Bonsai Collection are displayed on open concrete pedestals. Displayed to the right of the Japanese Maple are a Coast Redwood by artist Mr. Toichi Domoto, and a San Jose Juniper by artist Mr. Mas Moriguchi.*

Opposite Top Left *Creeping Juniper, cascade style.*
Artist: Mr. Umenori Hatanaka   Date of origin 1940, bonsai since 1940

Opposite Top Right *Tamarisk, weeping style, spring color, 26 inches high*
Artist: Mr. Richard Ota   Date of origin 1986, bonsai since 1986

Opposite Bottom Left *Catlin Elm, Broomstyle-Root over Rock, fall color, 28 inches high*
Artist: Mr. John Naka   Date of origin 1970, bonsai since 1970

Opposite Bottom Right *Firethorn, Informal Upright style, winter color, 24 inches high*
Artist: Mr. Cheen Chong Yea   Date of origin 1968, bonsai since 1970

Above Left *Japanese Larch, Group style, 24 inches high*
Artists: Mr. Taki Nagasawa and Mrs. Amy Liang Chang   Date of origin 1974, bonsai since 1976

Above Right *Chinese Juniper, Formal Upright and Semi-cascade Twin Trunk style, 36 inches high*
Artist: Mrs. Amy Liang Chang   Date of origin 1960, bonsai since 1962

KUBOTA GARDENS
Seattle, Washington

Twenty acre Kubota Garden had its beginning in 1927 as the family home of Fujitaro Kubota and for the base of his landscaping business. As Kubota's knowledge grew, the garden also grew, becoming a unique blend of traditional Japanese style and plant materials indigenous to the Northwest. Kubota's mastery of garden design is evident in the ingenious combinations of color, patterns and texture found in no other garden. The layout of the garden offers the delightful aspect of being left to explore in the direction of one's choosing. A mountainside trail, a necklace of ponds, a memorial stone, a bamboo grove, a hidden meditation spot missed by most; these secret corners of delight will unfold for those who pay attention.

Previous Page Left *Japanese iris grow along the waters edge near the vermilion moon bridge. Out of view at the pond's edge stands a large upright stone containing a large fossilized Giant Horsetail.* Right *The Kubota family channeled Mapes creek to create a necklace of ponds through the garden. A number of construction methods were used to span the waters. Long slabs of cut stone cross this waterway.*

Above *A view from Tom Kubota's Stroll Garden shows the infinite variety of trees that have reached maturity since the Kubota family began planting the site in the 1920's.*

Opposite Top *A waterfall plunges from this Lookout to the garden 65 feet below. The red railing of a bridge can be spotted far below.*

Opposite Bottom Left *Bridges of the Round Moon were built in China 2,500 years ago. These highly arched bridges, combined with their reflections, form a complete circle.* Center *An incredible 32 foot long Weeping Blue Atlas Cedar and a 37 foot high Weeping Norway Spruce act as a back drop for this sparse but effective arrangement of rocks.* Right *Fujitaro Kubota was 82 years old when this memorial stone was placed in the newly constructed Mountainside Garden. A brief history of the garden is contained on its carved face.*

WASHINGTON PARK ARBORETUM
Seattle, Washington

Washington Park Arboretum isn't popular just because it houses an internationally known collection of camellias, hollies, Japanese maples, and conifers. It's also popular because it welcomes visitors with wide grassy paths through breathtaking vistas of year-round displays.

Just as people flock to Japan to enjoy the cherry blossoms, garden lovers flock to Washington Park Arboretum to walk the long swards of Azalea Way when thousands of rhododendrons, azaleas and flowering trees burst into bloom each spring.

In summer, a popular destination is the waterfront trail at the north end of the arboretum that floats over peat bogs to provide a close up look at semi-aquatic plants and wildlife habitats. Lookout Gazebo will reward you with a territorial view of brilliant foliage in the fall, and the Joseph A Witt Garden displays a fine array of plants with winter interest.

Graham Visitor Center offers trail maps and pamphlets on plants of current interest, as well as a large selection of gardening books.

Left *Azalea Way in spring.*

Right *Molus Profusion*

Opposite Top Left *Davidia , a woodland tree from China, has showy white bracts that give rise to the common names dove tree, ghost tree or handkerchief tree.*

Opposite Top Right *A rhododendron bower forms as enchanting entry to one of the many side trails in the Arboretum.*

Opposite Bottom Left to Right *Evergreen Camellias bloom in early spring with white, pink or red flowers; The bright yellow flowers of Kirengeshoma palmata nod on their long slender stalks; flowering trees along Azalea Way.*

Above *The breathtaking beauty of a rhododendron.*

Above and Opposite Top Left *Quiet ponds in woodland settings give cause to pause in Washington Park Arboretum.*

Opposite Top Right *A fall scene along Azalea Way offers a moment to be treasured for a lifetime.*

Opposite Bottom Left *Much of the beauty of the Arboretum can be enjoyed on a pleasant drive that encircles its perimeter.*

Opposite Bottom Middle *A fall hike to Lookout Gazebo rewards one with a territorial view.*

Opposite Bottom Right *The B. O. Mulligan Sorbus Collection will surprise you with species that bear white, yellow and brown fruits, as well as the more common red and orange.*

THE JAPANESE GARDEN AT WASHINGTON PARK ARBORETUM
Seattle, Washington

Since the garden's design was implemented by Juki Iida in 1960, Washington Park's Japanese Garden has gracefully matured into a beautifully groomed retreat. Arranged as a stroll garden around a central lake, the design uses the technique of hide and reveal; composed views gradually unfold as one progresses along the path. Plantings of azaleas, camellias, flowering fruit trees and rhododendrons share the 2½ acre landscape with mosses, ferns, hostas and water plants. A beautiful wisteria trellis hangs heavy with bloom in spring. In fall the garden is ablaze with the changing colors of the Japanese maple, cherry, and dogwood trees.

The teahouse, hand crafted from a Japanese design, is built of cypress and cedar with a copper roof. It is enclosed by a mixed evergreen hedge in its own small garden and is used by students who study or participate in the tea ceremony.

Previous Page Left *Although Japanese gardens are not generally thought of as being colorful, there are times in spring when the flowering fruit trees and rhododendrons are breathtaking. The rock wall is capped with the brilliant red blooms of Rhododendron 'Arnoldianum'. A omakaga-gata lantern sits at the water's edge. On the hillside is the Kobe friendship lantern.* Right *Water lilies form a softening transition between the shore and pond.*

Above *The yukimi doro (lantern with a view of the snow) in the foreground is one of the most widely seen designs in Japanese gardens. It is most attractive when a few inches of snow have accumulated on its broad cap. The small island (nakajima) is reached by a plank bridge (yatsuhashi).*

Opposite top *A gently arching stone bridge spans a mountain stream. A todo gata lantern stands to the right of the bridge.*

Opposite Bottom Left *Rhododendron 'Arnoldianum'.*

Opposite Bottom Right *Turtles can often be seen sunning themselves on the rocks of this small island. Koi, frogs and herons may also be spotted in and around the pond.*

Above *A resident guard cat takes time from his duties for a nap.*

Left *Japanese iris, planted at the water's edge, have long, slender stems topped by huge, flat flowers.*

Opposite Top *A yukimi doro lantern nestles amongst willow and maple trees. Rhododendrons bloom in the back-ground.*

Opposite Bottom Left *Reflections repeat the lyrics of nature.*

Opposite Bottom Right *Look for plant combinations, such as rhododendrons and ajuga, that you can plant in your own garden. Choose plants with differences that bring attention to the best characteristics of each plant.*

MEDICINAL HERB GARDEN
Seattle, Washington

Located in the midst of the beautiful University of Washington campus, this two acre garden is the largest of its kind in the Western hemisphere. It serves as an invaluable source of information about herbaceous plants for both medicinal and domestic uses. As a result of a worldwide seed exchange program established in 1922, hundreds of specimens imported from around the world now mingle with the regional plants once used by Native Americans. Together they form a fascinating mixture of textures, colors, fragrances, blossoms and pods.

Since the gardens were established in 1911 they have undergone numerous changes in size and purpose. After enduring a period of neglect, the Friends of the Medicinal Herb Garden was formed to care for the gardens and educate the public about this most remarkable display of plants.

Previous Page Right *Sanguisorba canadensis, Canadian Burnet.*

Above and Opposite Right *As was often the case with herb gardens during the Renaissance and Baroque eras, the University gardens serve as a place of refuge and beauty as well as a practical place in which to grow medicinal or cooking herbs. The medicinal plants are arranged in square planting beds in seven interconnected gardens along Stevens Way. The gardens are surrounded by a diverse collection of mature trees and shrubs. Information tags identify both herbs and trees. A printed plant inventory may be purchased from the Friends of the Medicinal Herb Garden.*

Opposite Bottom Left *A wide variety of plants grow around the perimeter of the garden.*

Opposite Bottom Right *Eryngium amethystinum, Sea Holly. This clump forming herbaceous perennial is grown in zones 3-8 for it's steel-blue to amethyst flowers. Be sure to cut the stems before the flowers are fully open.*

Above Left   *The gardens are presently divided into several formal and informal areas and are enhanced by numerous species of mature trees including cascara, yews, fig, judas trees, holly, oak and dogwood. Here a flowering dogwood tree is doing everything it knows how to do all at once.*

Above Right   *These monkeys guard the garden and welcome visitors to Cascara Circle at the west end of the gardens. This grassy circular area, cut by a small stream, is surrounded by native plants.*

Opposite Top   *The beauty of a Ficus carica, common fig, growing in the west garden.*

Opposite Bottom, Left to Right   *Garden Angelica; an awesome 106 foot Sierra Redwood, or Giant Sequoia, standing guard in the midst of the garden; White Baneberry (Dolls Eyes).*

VOLUNTEER PARK CONSERVATORY
Seattle, Washington

Victorian style Volunteer Park Conservatory opened to the public in 1912. It is perfectly placed at the end of a long avenue of trees in 45 acre Volunteer Park.

The conservatory is divided into five areas, each with temperature and humidity controls appropriate for the displays of Bromeliads, Ferns, Palms, Cactus and seasonal plants. Many of the conservatory's plant collections were either started or augmented by donations of rare and unusual plants by patrons.

During a renovation in the early 1980's, artist Richard T. Spaulding designed and executed a stained glass entry canopy that welcomes visitors with glass panels showing a history of architectural ornamentation.

Above *Fruit of the prickly pear.*

Opposite *A fine collection of rare and unusual orchids is housed on one side of the Palm House. Their exotic blooms make them a desirable ornamental indoor plant. Many of the hybrids are easier to grow than one might think.*

Opposite Top Right *Cycads fill the center of the Palm House. Cycads, probably the most primitive of living seed bearing plants, are found in almost all tropical and sub-tropical environments from arid to rain forest. Indigenous peoples have found ways to bypass the poisons they contain to make such foods as 'seminole bread' and 'tortilla meal'.*

Above Left *Caladium are grown for their beautiful bicolor leaves.* Right *The leaves of this bromeliad form cups that collect rain water.*

Right *A pond of goldfish is a fun distraction for children of all ages.*

These 2 Pages *The Cactus House. Because of the adverse conditions they endure in their natural habitats, cacti and other succulents grow in a fascinating array of shapes and forms. Their textures include smooth, waxy, hairy or spiny surfaces. Many have brightly colored flowers that enhance their appeal as houseplants. Common to all is the presence of water-storing tissue in the stems, roots and leaves that enable then to withstand long periods of drought.*

Above *Notocactus magnificus.*

Opposite Top Right *Plants include Cereus argentinensis, Agave parryi, and Carnegiea gigantea.*

Opposite Bottom Left *Notocactus Leninghausii.* Right *Myrtillocactus geometrizans crest.*

WOODLAND PARK ROSE GARDEN
Seattle, Washington

Woodland Park Rose Garden, one of 24 All-American Rose Selection (AARS) test gardens in the United States, opened in 1924. The 2½ acre garden houses over 5,000 roses of 260 varieties and receives more than 200,000 visitors a year.

Trees and architectural elements support the beauty of this structurally pleasing formal rose garden. Mature evergreens, deciduous trees and a tall wrought iron fence of simple integrity surround the garden and provide a comfortable sense of enclosure. The lines of the garden are given visual impact by rows of clipped oriental cypress and intersecting paths that lead to a central axis, a raised birdbath planter with a canopy of flowering trees overhead.

113

Types of roses grown at Woodland Park Rose Garden include hybrid teas, floribundas, grandifloras, miniatures, old garden roses, climbers, landscape, tree roses and David Austens.

Because roses are not particularly attractive in winter, care must be taken when planning a rose garden to add interest and structure that will carry the garden through this period. Surrounding the garden with an evergreen hedge such as yew or adding a short clipped boxwood hedge around the beds will do much to correct the problem. Pergolas, pillars, latticework and sculptures add structure year round as do paths of brick, gravel or grass. The gazebo, birdbath planter, evergreens and paths all add interest to the Woodland Park Rose Garden

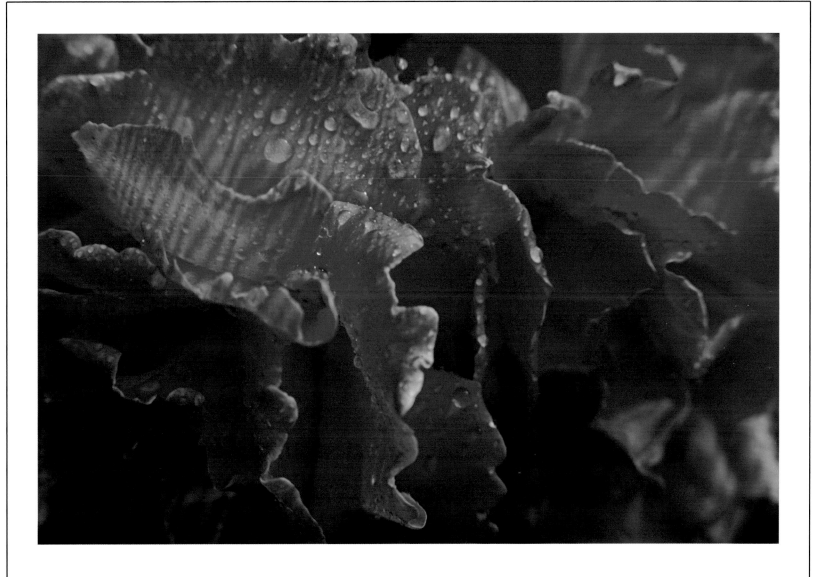

In 1947 the Woodland Park Rose Garden was selected as one of 24 AARS test gardens in the United States. Each year rose breeders supply these gardens with new roses that are judged spring and summer for two years by the garden staff. Based on criteria that includes disease resistance, color and fragrance, AARS selects up to four winners each year. The majority of the roses at Woodland Park Rose Garden are AARS winners. Winners are designated with a green metal sign stating the year of introduction.

THE BLOEDEL RESERVE
Bainbridge Island, Washington

The Bloedel family, who made the Reserve their home in 1951, was primarily responsible for the growth and development of the 150 acre property. With the help of designers, Thomas Church, Richard Haag and especially Geoffrey Rausch, they gradually and thoughtfully integrated garden spaces into their landscape. Mr. Prentice Bloedel's constant vision for the estate was the creation of a garden where people could contemplate the beauty and harmony of nature in a tranquil setting. The Arbor Fund, which now manages the Reserve, continues to care for the garden in the spirit of the Bloedel philosophy.

Your peaceful walk through the Bloedel Reserve will reveal a Rhododendron Glen, Japanese and Moss Gardens, the Bird Sanctuary, the Reflection garden, and the Residence Gardens surrounding the French style home. In the spirit of keeping the Bloedel philosophy intact, appointments are required to visit the garden.

Previous Page *The Visitor Center, formerly the Bloedel home. Roosters on either side of the entry gate welcome visitors to the Bloedel Reserve.*

Above and Opposite Bottom Center *The entrance gate and the Zen Garden were designed by Dr. Koichi Kawana. The stones, set in raked sand, appear to be islands in a sea. As with most meditation gardens, the surroundings are kept simple and neutral in design.*

Opposite Top *The Japanese Garden was designed and constructed by Fujitaro Kubota of Seattle in 1960-61. It is designed as a stroll garden with a central pond surrounded by Japanese maples, Japanese black and red pines and junipers.*

Opposite Bottom Left *The fruit of an empress tree growing near the Gate House.*

Opposite Bottom Right *A lawn scene.*

Above and Opposite Bottom Left *The Bird Refuge was created by removing 4,000 cubic yards of peat. The resulting hole filled with water leaving secure islands where nesting birds can raise their young. Plantings known to attract birds seeking food and cover were introduced. Rainbow trout were added to the pond to attract kingfishers, herons and an occasional eagle. Trumpeter swans and mute swans were introduced to the pond. All other birds come and go as they like.*

Opposite Page *The Moss Garden was defined from an idea presented to Mr. Bloedel by Mr. Richard Haag and Mr. Richard Brown in 1984. After clearing the area of salmonberry and weeds, 275,000 starts of Irish moss were planted, most of which has now been crowded out by natural moss. The skunk cabbage grows along a small drainage stream running through the garden.*

Opposite Top and Above Left *The Himalayan Birch Garden, designed by Geoffrey Rausch, is one of many contributions he has made to the Bloedel Reserve. Ferns and other moisture loving plants surround a small woodland pond near the path.*

Opposite Bottom Left *A yew hedge seems to hold back the forest as it frames the Reflection Pond. The nearly 200 foot long pond, built to take advantage of the level of the natural water table, is fed by springs. The curved benches are old buttress support beams from a Winslow shipyard.*

Opposite bottom Right *The rear of the Bloedel home faces a view of Puget Sound. Now used as the Visitor Center, the ground floor is open to the public. The library of gardening books is of special interest.*

Above Right *One of Bloedel Reserve's serene ponds in fall.*

BELLEVUE BOTANICAL GARDEN
Bellevue, Washington

Bellevue Botanical Garden, one of the newest Northwest gardens, has quickly become a major center for gardening activities. The garden was conceived when Cal and Harriet Shorts gave their seven acre estate to the city of Bellevue in the early 1980's. Additional land around the estate was purchased for the project and the 36 acre Bellevue Botanical Garden opened to the public in 1992.

The former Short residence, designed by Seattle architect, Paul Kirk, now houses the library, garden shop and meeting rooms in the visitor center. Its exterior is surrounded by a Waterwise Garden, a Fuchsia Garden, and a rilled water feature.

Of special interest throughout the year is the 200 foot long Perennial Garden that includes beds for both shade and sun loving plants. The beds, arranged by color, include rare and unusual plants. Flowering shrubs and small trees give structure to the sloping beds. Other areas not to be missed are an extensive Alpine Rock Garden, Yao Oriental Garden, Ground Cover Garden, and a woodland walk featuring native plants.

Previous Page Left *The Puget Sound Dahlia Society maintains a Summer Dahlia Garden along this wide sidewalk where visitors can easily enjoy the colors, sizes and shapes of the diverse blooms.* Right *A rustic fence complete with finials decorates the perennial garden.*

Above and Opposite Top Left *The Eastside Fuchsia Society Maintains this beautiful test garden for the enjoyment and education of visitors who might like to grow fuchsias.*

Opposite Top and Bottom Right *This architectural water feature is integrated into the courtyard at the visitor center. Recirculating water flows from the stones in the foreground, through a rill in the brick plaza, to the pond in the distance.*

Opposite Bottom Left *A frog sculpture, donated by artist, Lon Busselback, is a donation bank.*

Above *The terrace at the Information Center looking toward the Perennial Garden.*

Opposite Top *Late season hot perennials are a bright spot in the 200 foot long Perennial Garden, created and maintained by the Northwest Perennial Alliance. Perennials are the most diverse plant group, with a wide range of color, form, shape, texture and fragrance. Ranging in height from ground covers to plants over eight-feet tall, they can stand alone in a border or blend with a mix of small trees, shrubs and annuals.*

Opposite Bottom Left and Center *A traditional Japanese gate marks the entrance to Yao Garden. A blend of Pacific Rim and Northwest plants fill this serene garden planted in honor of the sister city relationship between Yao, Japan and Bellevue.*

Opposite Bottom Right *Opened in 1997, the Alpine Garden fills a rocky hillside with the sturdy plants that survive in high mountainous conditions of extreme temperatures, sharp winds and a short growing season.*

OHME GARDENS
Wenatchee, Washington

From a distance, Ohme Gardens appear as an emerald set high on the hillside above the Wenatchee Valley. The garden was started in 1929 by Herman Ohme and opened to the public ten years later. Over the years, the Ohme family continued the arduous task of transforming the barren hillside by moving hundreds of tons of rock, planting thousands of evergreen trees and blanketing the slopes with low-growing alpine plants. The desolate hillside has gradually given way to a quiet, restful alpine garden.

The visitor is greeted with nine acres of greenery and weathered rock formations wound through with brooks and fern bordered pools. The slopes are covered with a profusion of mountainous ground covers that bursts into a carpet of soft colored blossoms each spring. The beauty of this high mountain jewel is augmented by dramatic sweeping views of the distant mountains, and hawks circling the valley below.

Alpine gardens are often thought of as homes for green plants with a vast variety of textures, but for a short time each spring phlox, ajuga, allyssum, violas, iberis and dainthus throw aside this reputation to splash the hillsides of Ohme Garden with blankets of color. Later in the season, the awesome rock formations will catch your attention. Winding rock paths will lead you through shady groves of aspen, cedar, fir, hemlock, maple vine, pine and spruce to blue-green ponds and pools with trickling waterfalls. Squirrels, lizards, marmots or rabbits may catch your eye while jays, robins, flickers, chickadees and orioles sing the praises of the garden. You may want to brave the highest lookout point for plunging views of the valley below. If not, there is a rustic shelter offering a serene, peaceful, flat place to rest.

The inhospitable conditions of rocky mountainsides with thin soil, strong winds, freezing temperatures and snow in winter are the original home of the lovely alpines and rock plants that now grace the slopes of Ohme gardens. These plants have adapted over time to survive hostile conditions. One of the most noticeable of these adaptations is their ground-hugging, compact habit of growth. This small size means that almost any garden has room for them. The range of easy to grow alpines with beautiful foliage, flowers and textures is vast. All that's required is a sunny area with free-draining soil, and water.

MANITO PARK
BOTANICAL GARDENS
Spokane, Washington

Within the 90 acres of Manito Park lie a number of diverse gardens that have been constantly perfected since the Olmsted Brothers' landscape architectural firm was commissioned for a general design of Spokane's park system in 1907.

At the hub of these gardens is Gaiser Conservatory, enjoyed year round for its displays of tropical plants, cactus, orchids and seasonal displays. Facing the conservatory lies the vast Duncan Garden reminiscent of the formal parterre gardens of France. Geometric beds of colorful annuals surround the magnificent Davenport Fountain presiding at the garden's center.

The Perennial Garden lies behind the conservatory, bordered on one side by a Butterfly Garden and on the other by a long, rock Wall Garden. Beyond the wall is a formal Rose Garden filled with modern hybrids, miniatures, and old-fashioned roses.

Manito's serene Nishinomiya Japanese Garden is designed as an oriental stroll garden with a waterfall cascading to the central Koi Pond. The garden is especially beautiful when the trees and shrubs are heavy with spring blossoms or fall color.

Above Left *The Davenport Fountain decorates the center of Duncan Garden.*
Above *The Davenport Fountain as seen through a clipped entry to Duncan Garden.*
Opposite Top *A riot of tulips, one of the seasonal displays in Gaiser Conservatory.*
Opposite Bottom *Many varieties of lilac grace Manito Gardens with fragrant blooms each spring. The lilac is the official flower of Spokane.*

Above *A view across the Joel E. Ferris Perennial Garden to the Rock Wall Garden. Over 300 plant species grow in the three acre perennial garden with tremendous variations in color, texture, shape and size.*

Left *Spring color on the Rock Wall.*

Above *Fall color on the Rock Wall. The range of plants suitable for rock gardens is vast, with a wide variety of foliage and flowers.*

Right *Every year hundreds of butterflies (here a Painted Lady) are attracted to the cascade of flowering plants on the Rock Wall.*

Above *A Snow Viewing Lantern (Yukimi Doro), so called because it is most beautiful with a covering of snow on it's wide top.*

Left *A subtle water feature made from natural materials graces a corner of the garden.*

Above *The arched bridge is a dominate feature of Japanese gardens, and a traditional place for ceremonies. The beautiful brocaded carp (koi) that inhabit the pond have been bred for their color. They symbolize strength, wisdom and courage to the Japanese. Each May 5th, Boys Day, parents fly a carp-shaped flag for each of their sons in hope that they will someday possess these same fine qualities.*

Right *A serene fall view of the waterfall and stone pagoda in Nishinomiya Japanese Garden. The garden is named after Spokane's Sister City.*

UNIVERSITY OF BRITISH COLUMBIA BOTANICAL GARDENS

Vancouver, British Columbia

Set in a native west coast forest, vine-covered firs, hemlocks and cedars shelter the wide paths that wind through the under-story of the David C. Lam Asian Garden. Species rhododendrons, maples, viburnums, and hydrangeas share the cool forest floor while hostas, lilies, primulas and ferns thrive along the damp edges of streams that wind through the garden. Forest loving birds, attracted by seeds and berries, serenade visitors.

A stroll through Moongate Tunnel brings one to the Food Garden, Physick Garden, Arbour Garden, Native Garden and Winter Garden. One of the largest Alpine gardens on the continent sits on the sunny slopes in this area. The diverse collection of plants in these gardens, designed primarily for education, will delight as well as instruct.

Left   *Plantings of lilies, primulas, meconopsis, rodgersia and hostas are used as ground covers to help control weeds throughout the Asian Garden.*

Right   *A variety of vines find their niche in the native west coast forest of the Asian Garden.*

Above Left *The Canadian Big Leaf Maples put on a blazing show of color each fall.*

Above *Hydrangeas, as well as rhododendrons (opposite page bottom right) , roses and magnolias growing in the David C. Lam Asian Garden are all species plants that grow in the wild, rather than hybrids that have been cross-bred by plantsmen.*

Opposite Top *The David C. Lam Asian Garden, begun in 1975, houses plants form the temperate zones of China, Taiwan, the Himalayas and Japan.*

Opposite Bottom Left *When leaving the Asian Garden, the vine covered Moongate Tunnel gives safe passage under S. W. Marine Drive to several other gardens.*

Above Left and Opposite Bottom Left *Loniceria 'Dropmore Scarlet', pyracantha, clematis, kiwi, ivy, and roses are just a few of the vines growing throughout the gardens.*

Above Right *Many ornamental grasses and sedges are grown in both sun and shade at UBC Botanical Gardens.*

Opposite Top *Six-foot wide raised beds make up most of the ¾ acre Food Garden. Around the perimeter, fruit trees are trained in a variety of espalier methods.*

Opposite Bottom Right *By using black plastic to warm the soil and radiate heat onto the plants, UBC gardeners have great success with cantaloupe, a plant that is notoriously hard to grow in the Northwest.*

NITOBE MEMORIAL GARDEN
Vancouver, British Columbia

Nitobe Memorial Garden was dedicated in 1960 to the memory of Dr. Inazo Nitobe, a Japanese scholar and diplomat whose goal was to become a bridge across the Pacific. This 2½ acre Shinto garden was designed by Japanese landscape architect, Professor Kannosuke Mori. The peaceful stroll garden serves as a contemplative walking place where one reflects on life and the way of the gods as a preliminary to the tea ceremony.

In Japanese gardens, all things are imbued with either male or female spirits to depict a balance between masculine and feminine forces. Through an adept placement of these symbols, Nitobe Garden becomes an aesthetic composition of lessons and morals encountered on life's journey. The lanterns, plants, stones, and water seem to be naturally placed, but are actually integral parts of a symbolic walk meant to refresh and teach the spirit.

Left *Although the garden is beautiful year around, it is especially so in the spring when the Japanese Flowering Cherries and the azaleas are in bloom, and again in the fall when the leaves turn color. These subtle variations of nature serve to remind us of the seasons of our lives. The gardens six bridges represent significant changes in our lives.*

Right *Tree trunks and ground cover form an abstract pattern in Nitobe's woodland garden.*

Above Left *Nitobe Memorial Lantern (Father Lantern, Kasuga style). This stone lantern, one of the most striking features in the garden, is dedicated to the memory of Dr. Nitobe. It is said to be the axis of the world, holding up the sky. Its cosmic significance is shown by the sculptured signs of the zodiac below the lantern proper.*

Above Right *A view from the Family Viewing Pavilion toward the Island of Eternal Life. The turtle shaped island represents paradise and immortality.*

Opposite Top *Japanese Flowering Cherries in a springtime dance over the arched Earth Bridge and the Family Viewing Pavilion.*

Opposite Bottom Left *The placement of trees, shrubs and Stones along the shore of the Island of Eternal Life is intended to look as accidental as possible. The Snow-viewing lantern, Yukimi-doro, looks best with a blanket of snow on its cap.* **Opposite Bottom Right** *Cornus canadensis, a shade loving miniature dogwood spreads its white flowers over the forest floor in summer.*

VANDUSEN BOTANICAL GARDEN
Vancouver, British Columbia

Built on a former golf course site, this beautiful fifty-five acre garden was opened to the public in 1975. The topography of rolling hills with interconnecting lakes, streams and ponds provides the framework for a naturalistic landscape housing major plant collections from around the world. The collections are scientifically labeled and organized in aesthetic groupings that bring beauty to the garden and pleasure to the viewer. Display areas include a Sino-Himalayan Garden, Canadian Heritage Garden, Meditation Garden, Mediterranean Garden, Alma VanDusen Perennial Garden, Rose Garden and Rock Garden.

Left and Above *The infinite variety of VanDusen plants.*

Opposite *Rhododendron Walk.*

Above *Well placed metal cranes add impact to a garden vignette.*

Above Right *Entwined with mature vines, the entry porch frames a distant view of a lake fountain and gives a hint of horticulture delights to come.*

Right *The pink and white blossoms of cosmos add a bright touch of late summer color to the edge of this pond.*

Above and Left *Handsome sculptures are placed throughout the garden. Here, feeding geese echo the shape of their stone companion.*

Above Right *A small hexagonal shelter topped by a rooster weathervane delights those who visit the Children's Garden.*

Opposite Top *Water lilies cover this section of the extensive waterway that meanders through the garden.*

Opposite Bottom Left *Water lily.*

Opposite Bottom Right *Keeping a sharp eye on the banks of the streams will reap a sighting of herons, turtles and a myriad of other water life.*

Above *The Korean Pavilion.*

Left *Succulents form a pleasing pattern in a small wedge of earth.*

Right *Just a touch of color makes this composition sing.*

Opposite Top *A formal Rose Garden, neatly framed with boxwood, has crushed gravel paths and a central sculpture. The stone arch adds depth to the design. Surrounding the rose beds with boxwood gives them definition and enhances the garden's appearance, especially in winter.*

Opposite Bottom *The Elizabethan Maze invites adventure.*

QUEEN ELIZABETH PARK
Vancouver, British Columbia

The nearly six million people who visit the 130 acre Queen Elizabeth Park each year are treated to one of the most unique and beautifully maintained gardens in Canada. The gardens, built around an abandoned rock quarry, house seasonal displays of perennials and annuals. All of the trees native to Canada and many species from around the world grow there as well.

A gift of Prentice Bloedel, the conservatory perches on the crest of the park like a triodetic space ship come to display the exotic birds and plants gathered in its travels. Surrounding the conservatory are stunning views of the city and sculptures by J. Seward Johnson Jr. and Henry Moore.

Left *The large quarry garden in spring.*
Above *'The Photo Session', a sculpture by J. Seward Johnson, Jr.*

Opposite Top *The practice of inter-planting is ideal for those who leave their bulbs in the ground year round. The secondary plants add interest and beauty to the garden. One can echo color or use a complementary color. For luxuriant inter-planting with tulips try cowslips, glory of the snow, primulas, crocus, hyacinths or pansies.*

Opposite Bottom Left *An early morning visit will reward one with a quiet walk of stunning beauty.*

Opposite Bottom Right *A complementary planting of red and green tulips.*

Above Left *A bright tumble of tulips are a colorful surprise against the gray rocks and path.*

Above Right *Spring flowering groundcovers cling tenaciously to the side of the old quarry wall.*

Above *The 70 foot high triodetic dome of the Bloedel Conservatory encloses over 15,000 square feet of tropical, dessert, and temperate climates.*

Opposite Top *The interior of the conservatory has an open plan with circular paths that provide easy viewing of the plants, birds and animals. Brugmansia x versicolor, or Angle Trumpets, overhang the path and fill the air with the strong, tropical fragrance of its huge trumpet shaped blossoms.*

Opposite Bottom *These colorful birds seem to be natural comics with an ever-changing venue of entertainment.*

Above *Flowering bulbs, particularly tulips, are planted by the tens of thousands to complement the comprehensive collection of trees and shrubs throughout the garden.*

Opposite Top *A spectacular view of Vancouver seen from the overlook above the North Quarry Garden.*

Opposite bottom *A climb to the floor of the quarry rewards visitors with a view of the overlook bridge, and the waterfall cascading down the face of the cliff.*

DR. SUN YAT-SEN CLASSICAL CHINESE GARDEN
Vancouver, BC

Dr. Sun Yat-Sen Garden, styled after the Suzhou gardens of southern China, is the first full-scale garden of it's kind to be constructed outside of China. The garden was completed in 1986 under the direction of master architects Mr. Wang Zu-Xin, chief architect, and Mr. Fen Xiao Lin from China; and Joe Wai, architect, and Don Vaughn, landscape architect, from Vancouver, BC. For more than a year fifty-two Suzhou craftsmen labored to assemble the architectural elements shipped from China.

In spite of the fact that the garden covers only half a city block, artfully placed elements within the garden, as well as borrowed views from the adjacent park, give the illusion of a much larger space.

Typical of Suzhou classical gardens constructed during the Ming Dynasty (1368-1644), the Dr. Sun Yat-Sen Classical Chinese Garden exhibits four characteristic features: water, stone sculptures, buildings and plants. These elements are arranged with a large pond and an open pavilion (ting) atop a false mountain as the dominant theme in the garden. The main hall and scholar's study along with high white walls and open corridors surround the central garden and move the viewer from one scenic view to another.

Left *A view of the Water Pavilion from the adjoining Dr. Sun Yat-Sen Park.*

Above *A lattice-work moon gate on one side of the open Water Pavilion frames a borrowed view of the adjacent park. Traditionally, the lattice-work is done in either a geometric or floral design.*

Opposite Top Left *Large eroded stones form the entrance to a water cave beneath the false mountain and pavilion.*

Opposite Top Right *Presiding atop the false mountain, a hexagonal pavilion (ting) serves as a place to rest and observe scenery. The soaring wings of the roof are a lively expression of classical Chinese garden architecture. The false mountain is constructed of earth and large eroded stones that also form the water cave at the rear of the structure.*

Opposite Bottom Left *A pleasing contrast of materials exists between the cut stone landing, the natural stone step and the geometric stone pattern of the courtyard.*

Opposite Bottom Right *Probably the single most striking element in the garden are the eroded rocks that form vertical sculptures, false mountains, caves and edging for pools.*

Above *There are no lawns in the garden. Instead, courtyards are paved with intricately hand set stone mosaics in geometric and abstract floral designs. Clay roof tiles are used to edge planting areas.*

Opposite Top *White walls act as a foil for arrangements of stones and plants in the scholar's courtyard. The courtyard and adjoining study are reserved for the master of the house.*

Opposite Bottom Left *Detail of Lattice Moongate.*

Opposite Bottom Middle *Entrance to the Dr. Sun Yat-Sen Park.*

Opposite Bottom Right *This small entrance garden serves as a transition from the busy street to the main garden. It's small tracery window gives a hint of what is to come. The traditional hexagonal floor pattern is hand set with small oblong colored stones.*

DR. SUN YAT-SEN

PARK AND TILFORD GARDENS
North Vancouver, British Columbia

Originally established in the late 1960's by a distillery, Park and Tilford gardens attracted many visitors before falling into ruin when the business closed. After a major renovation, the gardens reopened in 1989. Today horticulture students from Capilano College receive landscaping and grounds maintenance skills at the garden with the best students being hired as summer gardeners.

Park and Tilford proves that, with careful planning, big ideas can be successfully executed in small spaces. This intimate 2½ acre garden, tucked into a quiet corner of the shopping center, integrates eight different garden styles so that each garden flows cohesively into the next. Because of their residential size they serve as a ready source of inspiration for the home gardener. Garden styles represented at Park and Tilford include Native, Herb, Rose, Oriental, Colonnade, Rhododendron, and White.

Previous Page *Repetition of curved lines lends a cohesive element to this Rhododendron Garden near the entry to Park and Tilford Gardens. The colorful spring bulbs enhance the blooms of the rhododendrons. Later on, the bulbs will be lifted and replaced with summer flowering plants.*

Above *Fallen blossoms from the flowering trees float across the blue tiled pool that serves as a focal point in the Colonnade Garden.*

Opposite Top *Park and Tilford's Rose Garden is enclosed by high, vine covered walls that give the space definition. The rose beds are defined with a lavender hedge.*

Opposite Bottom Left *The seed heads of the clematis are as beautiful as its flowers.*

Opposite Bottom Right *Rosa 'Summer Fashion'.*

Opposite Top *A view across the White Garden toward the Colonnade Garden shows how the trees are trimmed to allow light to permeate the space as filtered shade.*

Opposite Bottom Left *The lines of this sturdy wooden trellis are softened by a tumble of purple clematis.* Right *Short lived but spectacular poppy blooms.*

Above Left *A White Garden is the perfect answer for those who enjoy their gardens in the evening. White gardens shine in late day or in moonlight. Residential white gardens look best in a small, enclosed, partially shaded area surrounded by a supportive framework of foliage. The pleasant sound of a fountain and fragrant plants such as nicotiana, viburnum, lilacs and flocks will add a seductive dimension.*

Above Right *A variety of Japanese maples, ferns, mosses, pines and a small collection of bamboo surround the koi pond in this Oriental Contemplation Garden. Attention to scale was essential in the creation of this small space that feels larger than it is.*

THE BUTCHART GARDENS
Victoria, British Columbia

The history of this renowned garden dates from 1904 when the Vancouver Portland Cement Company was founded and Mrs. Butchart began planting flowers and shrubs around their nearby home. By 1906 the garden had expanded to include the area that is now the Japanese Garden. Soon after, Mrs. Butchart hired a head gardener and Mr. Butchart supplied labor from the cement plant. Word of the expanding garden and Mrs. Butchart's' hospitality spread. In 1915 tea was served to 18,000 visitors. Over the years the family has maintained a commitment to horticulture and hospitality that draws delighted visitors from around the globe.

The 50 acre garden includes a Sunken Garden, Rose Garden, Japanese Garden, Italian Garden, Star Pond Garden and Ross Fountain Garden, as well as a concert lawn, a fireworks basin and a show greenhouse. These beautifully orchestrated gardens offer a pageant of vivid color for every season, as outdoor concerts, fireworks displays and Christmas carolers entertain visitors throughout the year. During the summer the gardens are lighted for night viewing.

Opposite Left and This Page Left *Ross Fountain, completed in 1964 to commemorate The Butchart Gardens' 60th anniversary. The water, rising 75 feet in ever-changing patterns, is illuminated at night.*

Opposite Right *Hot colors and cool waters in the Italian Garden.*

Above *Old trees arch their cool shade over the verdant lawn while light-hearted plantings dance around their bases and skip along the path.*

Upper Left '*The Three Sturgeons*', *a classical bronze fountain cast in Florence, Italy.*

Above Right '*A Girl With a Fish*', *a lead fountain in the Italian Garden.*

Lower Left The *Butchart Gardens are well known for their array of annuals and perennials in daring color combinations.*

Above *The Sunken Garden is built on the former site of a limestone quarry. This garden is filled with beautiful specimens of old trees surrounded by lush beds of seasonal flowers.*

Above *A rustic arbor covered with climbing roses provides a shady retreat in the rose garden.*

Opposite Top Left *Lush plantings of begonias surround a playful putti fountain whose single spurt lends a lyrical splash to the lily pond.*

Opposite Bottom Left *Variegated ivy leaves are echoed in shadow as they encircle a large clay pot on a sunny veranda.*

Opposite Right *'A Girl With a Fish' fountain reigns supreme over the cross-shaped lily pond of the Italian Garden.*

HATLEY PARK GARDENS

Victoria, British Colombia

Hatley Park was originally the 650 acre estate of James Dunsmuir, a coal and railroad tycoon and Lieutenant Governor of British Columbia (1906-1909). It now serves as the impressive setting for the Royal Roads University. The 200 foot long sandstone castle is dominated by an 82 foot high turret. Many of its accouterments, including stained glass windows, pewter light fittings and exotic woods, were imported.

The Formal Italian Garden serves as the opulent background for the castle. Its gracefully curving pergola is shaded by roses, clematis and wisteria, some of which are over 85 years old.

Three small spring-fed lakes form the backbone for the Japanese Garden. Many of the original cherry, maple and umbrella pines still grace the strolling style garden, as do beautiful plantings of rhododendron.

The Rose Garden has a formal composition with the original Dunsmuir sundial gracing its center. Nearby is a naturalized English Garden and lagoon.

Left and Right
*Hatley Park
entrance gardens.*

193

These Two Pages *Original urns and statues of the four seasons are framed by boxwood hedges and the intersecting pattern of brick pathways in the Italian Garden. A pergola, heavy with roses, runs along one side of the garden. An ivy-draped lion spurts water into a water lily pond. The ivy covered stairs lead to the croquet lawn.*

Above and Opposite *The serene Japanese Garden, covering four acres, surrounds three spring-fed lakes. The original Japanese maples and Japanese cherries still grow in the garden, providing stunning color in spring and fall.*

Left *Hydrangeas brighten up the English Lagoon Garden in late summer.*

Opposite Top Left *Ferns, hostas and primulas form a study of texture in the Japanese Garden.*

Opposite Top Right *A small bridge under a colorful canopy of spring trees.*

Opposite Bottom Left *A red dragon fly takes a sun bath.* Right *Succulents and poppies.*

Above *An open hexagonal hut provides shelter from the elements for garden visitors.*

MINTER GARDENS
Rosedale, British Columbia

Since its inception in the late 1970's, Minter Gardens, a 27 acre masterpiece set in a fertile valley below Mt. Cheam, has achieved status as one of Canada's major visitor attractions.

As each theme garden opens before you, you'll discover one impeccably designed botanical delight after another. Spring brings forth thousands of tulips, daffodils and hyacinths with a snowstorm of blossoms from the hundreds of cherry, plum, magnolia and dogwood trees, as well as rhododendrons. Summer bursts upon the scene with a show-stopping presentation of annuals, perennials and vines that bloom until the trees become a blaze of color against the snowy backdrop of Mt. Cheam. One needn't worry about when to visit Minter Gardens. It's always beautiful.

Previous Page Left *Every year Minter gardeners paint floral pictures to celebrate Canadian life. The scenes are wondrous to view from a distance. Even more wondrous is a close-up discovery of the plants used to create the design.*

Previous Page Right *Dare to enter the Minter Maze. Everyone finds their way out…eventually…we think.*

Above *The Arbor Garden offers a shady retreat of vines, annuals and perennials.*

Left *Spring beauties.*

Opposite Top *A Floral Peacock struts his stuff in ever-changing colors as the seasons pass.*

Opposite Bottom *Roses, Minter chow line, Magnolias.*

Above Left and Right *A topiary Victorian couple pauses in a shady spot near the Waterwheel and Pond.*

Right *A floral scene celebrating Canadian history.*

Opposite Top *A bench invites visitors to pause at this walkway of hydrangeas.*

Opposite Bottom Left *A formal Rose Garden graces a bend in the garden path.*

Opposite Bottom Right Ornamental Cabbages in fall.

Opposite Top *Flowering trees, tulips and daffodils form a breathtaking tapestry of color each spring.*

Opposite Bottom *Parade of Tulips.*

Above Left *A viewing pavilion in the Chinese Garden.*

Above Right *These stairs lead to a gallery housing the largest collection of rock penjing outside of the Republic of China. Penjing depict scenes of nature on a small, flat container. The art of bonsai evolved from this art form.*

Right *Meditating Buddha.*

GARDEN ACCESS INFORMATION

Directions to the gardens are meant to be used in conjunction with an area map. Phone numbers may change. Updated information, maps, and directions can be obtained by an Internet search using the name of the garden.

Please treat the gardens with respect. They are not playgrounds. Many of the gardens request that animals be left at home.

GARDENS OF OREGON STATE

SHORE ACRES GARDEN
Cape Arago Highway
Coos Bay, Oregon
541-888-2472
8:00 am to Dusk. Parking fee.
Wheelchair accessible, information/gift store, restroom.
Seeing- eye dogs only.
Located on the Cape Arago Highway, 13 miles southwest of Coos Bay/North Bend and U. S. Highway 101.

OWEN ROSE GARDEN
North Jefferson Street at the Willamette River
Eugene, Oregon
541-682-5333
Open daily during daylight hours. No fee.
Restroom, wheelchair access.
Supportive associations: Volunteers in Parks 541-682-4845.
From I-5 North or South, take exit 194B, merging onto I-105. Take OR-99 North exit toward West Eugene. Immediately turn right onto Madison, take an immediate right onto West 5th and then an immediate left onto North Jefferson which leads into the garden.

HENDRICKS PARK RHODODENDRON GARDEN
Summit Avenue and Skyline Drive
Eugene Parks and Open Spaces 541-682 5333
Open during daylight hours. No fee.
Restroom, guided tours, partly wheelchair accessible.
Supportive associations: Friends of Hendricks Park, American Rhododendron Society.
From U. S. Highway 99 (Franklin Boulevard), turn south onto Walnut Street. Follow Walnut to Fairmount Boulevard and turn east onto Summit Avenue.

BUSH HOUSE AND ROSE GARDEN
600 Mission Street S. E.
Salem, Oregon 97302
Bush House Museum 503-363-4714, City of Salem Parks and Recreation 503-588-6261
Daylight hours. No fee.
Bush House Museum tours Tuesday through Sunday, March through September, 12 pm - 5 pm; October through April 2 pm - 5 pm. Fee.
Supportive associations: Bush House Auxiliary.
From I-5, take exit 253 onto Mission Street, continue west to the corner of Mission and 6th Street.

HISTORIC DEEPWOOD ESTATE AND GARDENS
1116 Mission Street S. E.
Salem, Oregon 97302
503-363-1825
Open Sunday through Friday, daylight hours (Saturdays are often reserved for public rentals). No fee.
House tours are available for a modest fee. Call for hours.
Supportive associations: Friends of Deepwood.
From I-5 take exit 253 onto Mission. Drive west on Mission, turn left onto 12th to the parking lot.

CRYSTAL SPRINGS RHODODENDRON GARDEN
Portland Oregon, S. E. 28th Avenue, one block north of Woodstock near Reed College.
Garden information 503-771-8386, Wedding information 503-256-2483.
Open daylight hours, admission fee charged between 10 am and 6 pm.
Restroom, water.
Supportive associations: Friends of Crystal Springs Rhododendron Garden, Portland chapter of the American Rhododendron Society, Master Gardeners.

PORTLAND CLASSICAL CHINESE GARDEN
N. W. 3rd and Everett, close to downtown Portland, Oregon in Chinatown/Old Town
503-228-8131
Open daily November through March, 10 am - 5 pm; April through October, 9 am - 6 pm. Fee.
Supportive associations: Portland Classical Chinese Garden members and volunteers.

INTERNATIONAL ROSE TEST GARDEN
400 S. W. Kingston
Portland, Oregon 97201
Open daylight hours. No fee.
Garden store 503-277-7033, restroom, wheelchair accessible.
Supportive associations: Portland Rose Society.
Located in Washington Park, from I-5 take I-405 exit to Highway 26 West, take the Zoo exit to Washington Park, bear right and follow signs through Washington Park.

THE JAPANESE GARDEN
611 S. W. Kingston Avenue
Portland, Oregon 97201
503-223-1321
Open every day except Thanksgiving, Christmas and New Years Day. October through March, 10 am (12 pm Monday) - 4 pm; April through September, 10 am (12 am Monday) - 7 pm. Fee.
Gift store, restroom, water.
Supportive associations: The Japanese Garden Society of Oregon.
From I-405 exit onto Highway 26 West, take the zoo exit, bear right and follow the signs through Washington Park.

PENINSULA PARK ROSE GARDEN
700 North Portland Boulevard
Portland, Oregon 97217
Open daylight hours. No fee.
Restroom.
From I-5 take Portland Boulevard exit 304 and travel three blocks east on Portland Boulevard to Albina Street.

GARDENS OF WASHINGTON STATE

LAKEWOLD GARDENS
12317 Gravelly Lake Drive S. W.
Tacoma, Washington 98499
253-584-4106 or 1-888-858-4106
Open April through September, Thursday through Monday 10 am - 4 pm; October through March, Friday through Sunday 10 am - 3 pm. Fee.
Restroom, garden shop, library, wedding and event rentals 253-584-6115, much is wheelchair accessible.
Supportive associations: Friends of Lakewold, volunteer opportunities.
From I-5 take exit 124 Gravelly Lake Drive, turn west and follow the signs for approximately one mile.

W. W. SEYMOUR BOTANICAL CONSERVATORY
316 South G Street
Tacoma, Washington 98405
253-591-5330
Open daily 10 am - 4 pm except Thanksgiving and December 25th. No fee.
Gift shop, event rentals 253-350-1000.
From I-5 take exit 133 (705 North/City Center), follow signs for 705 North/Schuster Parkway, get in right lane and take the Stadium Way exit, turn right at the stop light onto Stadium Way, turn left onto 4th street, follow 4th to G Street and turn right.

POINT DEFIANCE PARK GARDENS
5400 North Pearl
Tacoma, Washington 98407
253-591-5328
Open daylight hours. No fee.
Wedding and event rentals 253-350-1000.
From I-5 North of Tacoma, take Highway 16 West exit and follow the signs.

RHODODENDRON SPECIES BOTANICAL GARDENS
2525 South 336 Street
Federal Way, Washington 98003
253-838-4646
Open March through May 10 am - 4 pm, closed Thursday; June through February 11 am - 4 pm, closed Thursday and Friday. Fee.
Bathroom, gift shop 253-661-9377, wedding and event rentals.
Supportive associations: Membership, volunteer opportunities.
Located at the Weyerhaeuser Corporation Headquarters Campus. From Seattle take I-5 south, take exit 142A and travel east on Highway 18, take the Weyerhaeuser Way South exit and travel north following signs.

PACIFIC RIM BONSAI COLLECTION
33663 Weyerhaeuser Way South
Federal Way, Washington 98001
253-924-3153
Open June through February 11 am - 4 pm, closed Thursday and Friday; March through May 10 am - 4 pm, closed Thursday. No fee.
Tours, lectures, special exhibits, bathroom, adjacent gift shop.
Directions are the same as the Rhododendron Species Botanical Gardens.

KUBOTA GARDENS
Renton Avenue South and 55 Avenue South
Seattle, Washington
206-684-4584
Open daylight hours. No fee.
Wedding and event rentals 206-684-4081, garden events.
Supportive associations: Kubota Garden Foundation 206-725-5060, volunteers.
From the north on I-5: leave the freeway at Pacific Highway South/East Marginal Way exit 158, Turn Left onto Ryan Way, turn left onto 51st Avenue South, Turn right onto Renton Avenue South, Turn right onto 55th Avenue South.
From the South on I-5: leave the freeway at Martin Luther King Jr. exit 157, stay on Martin Luther King Jr. Way, Turn right onto Ryan Way, Turn left onto 51st Avenue South, Turn Right onto 55th Avenue South.

WASHINGTON PARK ARBORETUM
2300 Arboretum Drive East
Seattle Washington, 98112
206-543-8800
Open Daylight hours. No fee.
Graham Visitors Center, open every day 10 am - 4 pm, has a gift store, information and bathroom, educational programs, plant sales and event rentals of Graham Visitor Center.
Supportive associations, Arboretum Foundation (membership and volunteers 206-325-4510).
From downtown Seattle: drive east on Madison Street to Lake Washington Boulevard East, turn left into the Arboretum.
From I-5: take exit 168 Bellevue-Kirkland onto Highway 520, take first exit onto Lake Washington Boulevard East and follow it into the Arboretum.
From east of Lake Washington: drive west on the Evergreen Point Bridge (highway 520), exit onto Lake Washington Boulevard South, from the ramp turn left into the Arboretum.

JAPANESE GARDEN AT WASHINGTON PARK ARBORETUM
Seattle, Washington
206-684-4743, ticket booth 206-684-4725
Open Tuesday through Sunday from March 1 through November 30. Opening time is 10 am, closing times vary with the season between 4 pm and 8 pm. Fee.
Tours, tea ceremonies, classes.
Supportive associations, Japanese Garden Society 425-861-7865.
Follow directions for Washington Park Arboretum.

MEDICINAL HERB GARDEN
University of Washington Campus
Seattle, Washington
206-543-1126
Open daylight hours. No fee.
Supportive associations, Friends of Medicinal Herb Garden.
Enter campus at the west gate on 15th Avenue N. E. and follow Stevens Way south and east to C-10 parking (Free on Saturday afternoons and Sundays). Other times, ask gate-keepers for nearest parking and a map.

VOLUNTEER PARK CONSERVATORY
1400 East Galer Street
Seattle, Washington
206-684-4743
Open every day including holidays from 10 am - 4 pm (7 pm in summer). No fee.
Gift store, guided tours, classes, plant sales.
Supportive associations: Friends of the Conservatory 206-322-4112.
From I-5: take Roanoke exit 168A east to 10th Avenue East, Travel south on 10th to Prospect Street, turn left and follow signs to Volunteer Park.

WOODLAND PARK ROSE GARDEN
700 North 50th
Seattle, Washington 98103
206-684-4863
Open daily 7 am - dusk. No fee.
Supportive associations: Seattle Rose Society.
From I-5: take N. E. 50th Street exit 169, travel west to Fremont Avenue North, turn right into pay parking lot (free during non-zoo hours).

THE BLOEDEL RESERVE
7571 East Dolphin Drive
Bainbridge Island, Washington 98110
206-842-7631
Restroom and water at the Gate House, some wheelchair access, maps .
Open Wednesday through Sunday, except federal holidays, from 10 am - 4 pm. RESERVATIONS REQUIRED. Fee.
Please leave all pets at home. Directions are given at the time of your reservation.

BELLEVUE BOTANICAL GARDEN
12001 Main Street
 Bellevue, Washington 98005
425-452-2750
Open daily 7:30 am - dusk. No fee. Visitor center open 9 am - 4 pm.
No pets in the garden.
Visitor Center, garden shop, library, restroom, water.
Supportive associations: Bellevue Botanical Garden Society, Northwest Perennial Alliance, Eastside Fuchsia Society.
From I-405: take the NE 8th Street exit, travel east, turn right onto 120th Avenue, turn left onto Main Street and go three blocks to the garden.

OHME GARDENS
3327 Ohme Road
Wenatchee, Washington 98801
509-662-5785   www.ohmegardens.com
Spring and fall hours are 9 am - 6 pm daily, Memorial Day weekend through Labor Day weekend hours are 9 am - 7 pm daily. Fee.
Restroom, gift shop, maps, and picnic area (no food or pets in the garden), accommodations for weddings.
The gardens are located just north of Wenatchee near the junction of highway 2 and 97A, up on the bluff, look for signs.

MANITO PARK BOTANICAL GARDENS
4 West 21st Street
Spokane, WA
509-625-6622
Open daylight hours. No fee.
Bathroom, meeting room, weddings, Conservatory Christmas lights.
Supportive associations: Friends of Manito 509-456-8038, volunteers.
From downtown Spokane: take Stevens Street going South, stay in far right lane merging onto Bernard and turn left on 21st Avenue.

GARDENS OF BRITISH COLUMBIA

UNIVERSITY OF BRITISH COLUMBIA BOTANICAL
GARDENS
6804 S. W. Marine Drive
Vancouver, British Columbia V6T 1Z4
604-822-9666
Open daily 10 am - 6 pm with shorter hours in winter. Fee.
Garden store, restroom, rental facilities (604-822-4804),
courses and lectures.
Supportive associations: UBC Botanical Garden Members.
From I-5: take S.W. Marine Drive westbound directly to the
park.

NITOBE MEMORIAL GARDENS
University of British Columbia
Vancouver, British Columbia
Gatehouse 604-822-6038
Open daily 10 am, seasonal closure at 5 pm - 6 pm. Fee.
Bathroom at Asian center across road, group visits, guided
tours, wedding rentals.
Located on the UBC campus near the Anthropology Museum
on Memorial Road.

VANDUSEN BOTANICAL GARDENS
5251 Oak Street
Vancouver, British Columbia V6M 4H1
604-878-9274
Open daily 10 am - dusk. Fee.
Wheelchair accessibility, Cart tours for visitors with limited
mobility, garden shop, library, restaurant, restroom, flower and
garden show, lectures, December Festival of Lights. Guide
dogs only.
Supportive associations: VanDusen Botanical Garden
Association.
Located at 37th Avenue and Oak Street. From USA: follow
Highway 99 (changes to Oak Street) to 37th Avenue and turn
Left.

QUEEN ELIZABETH PARK
33rd Avenue at Cambie Street
Vancouver, British Columbia
604-257-8584
Open daily dawn to dusk. No fee. Bloedel Conservatory open
daily except December 25th , Summer weekdays 9 am - 8 pm,
Summer weekends 10 am - 9 pm, winter 10 am - 5 pm. Fee.
Conservatory store, some wheelchair access, restroom, water.

DR. SUN YAT-SEN CLASSICAL CHINESE GARDEN
578 Carrall Street
Vancouver, British Columbia V6B 5K2
604-662-3207, infoline 604-299-9000 (#7133)
www.vancouverchinesegardens.com
Seasonal hours: opens 10 am, closes 4:30 pm - 7 pm. Closed
December 25 and January 1st . Closed Mondays November 1
through April 31st. Fee.
Guided tours, event rentals, gift shop, musical events.
Supportive associations: Membership, volunteer opportunities.
Located downtown in Chinatown at the corner of Carrall and
Keefer, near Stadium Sky Train.

PARK AND TILFORD GARDENS
440-333 Brooksbank Ave
North Vancouver, British Columbia V7J 3S8
604-984-8200
Open daily 9:30 am - dusk. December for Christmas Lights,
9:30 am - 9:30 pm. No fee.
Restroom. Mostly wheelchair accessible, restaurants in
shopping center.

BUTCHART GARDENS
800 Benvenuto Avenue, Brentwood Bay
Victoria, British Columbia
250-652-5256   www.butchartgardens.com
Opens 9 am daily (1 pm Christmas day) seasonal closings
between 3:30 pm and 10:30 pm. Fee.
Restaurant, garden shop, Christmas lights, fireworks,
entertainment, wheelchairs available on first come basis,
complementary storage lockers.
Tsawwassen to Swartz Bay Ferry: From Swartz Bay take
Highway 17 south, turn right onto McTavish Road, turn left
onto West Saanich (Highway 17A) and drive south for about
5.5 miles, turn right onto Benvenuto Avenue.
From Victoria: travel 14 miles north on Highway 17, turn left
onto Keating Road and continue for 5.5 miles, or take a tour
bus.

HATLEY PARK GARDENS
Royal Roads University
2005 Sooke Road
Colwood District
Victoria, British Columbia
250-391-2600   www.royalroads.ca
Open daily 10 am - 4 pm. No fee.
The museum (250-391-2600 ex 4456) in the lower level of
Hatley Castle is open afternoons from 1 pm - 4 pm. There
is a Christmas house tour at 1:30 pm the Sunday before
Christmas.
Supportive associations: Friends of Hatley Park Society
From downtown Victoria: follow Highway 1A (Gorge Road, a
left turn off Douglas Street) west as it follows the Esquimalt
Harbor. Continue southwest to the junction with Goldstream
and Highway 14 (Sooke Road), stay on Highway 14. Royal
Roads University is on your left.

MINTER GARDENS
52892 Bunker Road
Rosedale, British Columbia V0X 1X0
604-792-3799 mid-October through March
604-794-7191 April to mid-October
Toll free in North America 1-888-646-8377
Open daily April through mid-October: April and October 10
am - 5 pm, May and September 9 am - 5:30 pm, June 9 am
- 6 pm, July and August 8:30 am - 7 pm. Fee.
Pre-booked tours, restaurant, garden shop, entertainment,
wedding facilities, restroom.
Travel on Highway 1 about 90 minutes East of Vancouver,
British Columbia to exit 135. Signed.

INDEX

Give an autographed gift of EMERALD JOURNEY to your friends.

Yes, please send _____ autographed copies of Emerald Journey for $37.00 each (US funds) to :

Name _____

Address _____   _____

Include $4.95 shipping and handling for one book, and $2.95 for each additional book to the same address. Washington state residents add $3.00 sales tax per book. Make check or money order payable to Carolyn Starner and send to Carolyn Starner, 1907 East Desmet Ave, Spokane, WA 99202 USA. Print Clearly. Allow 3 weeks for delivery.